Iaroslav Wise

Inspirational Calendar Book

"Inspirational Calendar Book" consists of 366 short poems for each day of the year. Their purpose is to help maintain a positive, Christian, wise and harmless outlook in studies, work and everyday life. The author hopes that these poems will brighten not only readers' day, but also the day of those with whom they wish to share. The poems in this book can be read one poem a day or any number of poems can be read any time anywhere in the book. To help readers search poems by topic, the key words (index / tags) are provided at the end of the book.

Wise, I. (2021). *Inspirational calendar book.* Calgary, AB: Edocation Corp.

ISBN 978-1-989531-32-7

Format: book (paperback)
Language: English
Written & designed by: Iaroslav Wise
Published by: Edocation Corp.
Disclaimer: this book is published as has been submitted by the author and in the original languages

Acknowledgements

Thank God.

Thank you to my family for their loving support.

Thank you to readers for using and sharing these poems.

Table of contents

WINTER

January 1

A new year has started!
May God's blessings be with us;
From His commandments may our heart be never departed –
May we win in any good thing thus!
Thursday 31.12.2020

January 2

In any adventures that happen in life,
Be it winning a prize or facing a strife,
The Lord is with you.
May your words and deeds remain true.
Friday 01.01.2021

January 3

The things you encounter
Are sometimes hidden "under a counter"
By those who are not truthful or fear,
But you call things by their names; be wise and clear.
Friday 01.01.2021

January 4

Let your smile shine;
Let your faith be bright;
Let your hope glow and not decline;
Let our love grow and be in sight!
Friday 01.01.2021

January 5

A good way to advertise
Good deeds
Is to practise them, guys.
Therefore, to crop a fine harvest, plant good seeds.
Friday 01.01.2021

January 6

Not all good intentions are needed;
Therefore, not all requests are to be heeded.
Exercise wisdom, patience and cheer;
Invest in what is truly dear.
Friday 01.01.2021

January 7

Like Zootopia Judy and Nick, be smart.
This is going to help with your finish and start.
Couple that with hard work on a par
And you won't go near, you'll go far.
Friday 01.01.2021

January 8

Tough as it may be, remember to smile:
This will help you be agile;
Take your mind away from some things for a while;
Connect with others easier and cover a mile.
Friday 01.01.2021

January 9

Being an optimist means
Seeing the brighter side,
However tough it seems,
And preserving hope, however long is the ride.
Saturday 02.01.2021

January 10

Thinking positively is healthy truly.
It also helps achieve
Good goals in work and studies fully;
Crack tasks when others leave – believe.

Saturday 02.01.2021

January 11

Be of good cheer,
Whether you go far or near;
This helps in all,
Whether you study, work or play ball.

Monday 04.01.2021

January 12

It suffers long and is kind;
It believes all things
And leaves all unimportant ones behind:
Love! It carries upon wings…

* See also 1Cor. 13.

Monday 04.01.2021

January 13

The Lord is with you – worry not,
Even when debates are hot;
When you are unsure.
Believe, God is Strong to make you come ashore.
Wednesday 06.01.2021

January 14

Faith, hope and love are the Christian strength.
They help in all business, each day.
Stock up with those alway.
They help win and protect at length.
Wednesday 06.01.2021

January 15

At the start of every day remember to pray
To fulfill more and hit the core,
Whether you make hay or engage in stock exchange play;
Put it fore, achieve and thank, do not ignore.
Wednesday 06.01.2021

January 16

Whatever honest craft
You specialize in –
It can be your saving raft
Against hunger and boredom – do not give in.
Saturday 09.01.2021

January 17

Your occupation
Is the friend that does not betray.
Invest your time in it, in education –
That keeps a lot of misfortunes at bay.
Saturday 09.01.2021

January 18

In your work have a vision,
In studies and business too:
This helps direct efforts with precision
And achieve your goals all the way through.
Saturday 09.01.2021

January 19

As much as possible, avoid relying
On others in all.
May your heart be toward wisdom inclining.
God is the Only One Who will always hear your call.
                    Monday 11.01.2021

January 20

If possible, abide in peace with all.
Only let your heart be faithful like that of Ruth;
Let your lips pronounce wisdom and the truth;
Let your heart be brave, your mind cool, your ego small.
          * See also the Bible (Rom 12:18; Ru 1-4).
                    Monday 11.01.2021

January 21

When you work with people, such as a client in any domain,
Document all things –
So that if they do complain,
Their hands are bound with their own decisions and inaction as
if with rings.
                    Monday 11.01.2021

January 22

Speaking much
Leads to the consequences which are such
That none appreciates;
Therefore, be quick to listen and guard your mouth gates.
See also Pr. 10:19; Jam. 3:2-12.
Friday 15.01.2021

January 23

What is faith without kind deeds?
It is like speech which never feeds;
Like petal armour that protects no one.
Only those who used faith for acts of love and compassion won.
See also Jam. 2:14-26.
Friday 15.01.2021

January 24

In early morning and late night,
Rejoice with all your inner might,
For God gave you so much for that:
Thank, live, laugh, love – do not forget.
See also Php. 4:4.
Friday 15.01.2021

January 25

Be quick to listen, ami(e);
Slow to speak – believe me.
Our anger is not always right;
Open your mind and heart to light.
See also Jam. 1:19-20.
Friday 15.01.2021

January 26

When we ask in a prayer,
It should be with faith and hope –
Find those under the doubt layer.
When you study or work and in all – God is Strong to help you cope.
See also Mt. 21:22; Jam. 1:5-8.
Friday 15.01.2021

January 27

God recompenses for good deeds – for sure.
Therefore, avoid doing less, do more.
Where needed only, however, they should be applied;
The giver's hand is to be richly supplied.
See also Lk. 6:38.
Friday 15.01.2021

January 28

God sends victories and strength:
Abide with Him in your heart and deeds at length.
Because you are with Him – give up your worry;
He can turn all your hardships to your glory.
Saturday 16.01.2021

January 29

There is no happiness in worry;
There is also no use in it.
Whether you fly a spaceship or drive a lorry:
Rely on God in studies, work and rest – stay fit.
Saturday 16.01.2021

January 30

It is next to impossible to achieve
It all in one go.
Procrastination and frustration may make you want to leave.
Therefore, consistent work is the shortest way to grow.
Tuesday 19.01.2021

January 31

Big wins are rare;
Fair achievements through hard work are not.
"Big" and "quick" are the things we hear about a lot,
But you be the steady instead – take good care.
Tuesday 19.01.2021

February 1

Be thankful and happy about little things too:
Your breakfast, a day off, your study breakthrough.
Let your small achievements lead
To bigger ones, happiness, calmness and more, indeed.
Tuesday 19.01.2021

February 2

Those who work also need rest,
Whether they study to pass a test
Or are on a new job, –
In order to have strength and cheer and not to sob.
Thursday 21.01.2021

February 3

How much is determined by person's gratitude:
Manners, intellectual altitude,
Ability to appreciate,
The true greatness, skills to communicate!
Thursday 21.01.2021

February 4

We tend to think about pets
As if they were the liabilities of ours:
All those care items, food, vet hours…
In fact, they contribute to our health – they are assets.
Thursday 21.01.2021

February 5

Only a mind that's shallow
Rejects faith, my dear fellow.
There are some that are oblivious and are prone to correction,
And there are those that persist in the rejection.
Thursday 21.01.2021

February 6

Is it a good idea to call people by their names?
It, certainly, is if you respect their individuality claims;
If you consider yourself educated
And want a positive image of you in their eyes created.
Friday 22.01.2021

February 7

Do not underestimate your little grey cells,
Regardless of what one tells.
In every situation those should be deployed
To help determine what is good and what is void.
Friday 22.01.2021

February 8

Haste makes waste.
Even if someone says
The task is as easy as "copy & paste" –
Avoid, if you do not want to be the one who pays.
Sunday 24.01.2021

February 9

Take your time
To reflect on any important matter
If you do not wish to get a lime
Or to get fatter.

Sunday 24.01.2021

February 10

No use or need
Crying over spilled milk –
Get a cat to feed.
Turn the "rug" into "silk"

Sunday 24.01.2021

February 11

Have you seen a person who is active
In studies and work and is selective
About spending time?
Such a person is going to earn a degree and a gold dime.

January 2021

February 12

Do not get too attached to your PC
Neither your phone or anything at all:
These things may cause issues that even science cannot foresee–
Stay free; keep computer time small.
Friday 29.01.2021

February 13

Praise the Lord –
Whatever you can or cannot afford;
In studies and work, in deed and in word –
Praise the Lord!
Saturday 30.01.2021

February 14

There is a blessing in a smile –
Whether your cheek is plump or has a dimple –
Keep it sincere and simple.
It helps all be agile.
Saturday 30.01.2021

February 15

When you win a bunch
Or lose a ton,
Stay humane and do not hold a grudge;
Love, be humble – good and bad luck may soon be gone.
Saturday 30.01.2021

February 16

What do you need to cope?
First, remember that God loves you;
Therefore, have faith and courage, hope.
Pray, be steady in work, keep your distractions few.
Saturday 30.01.2021

February 17

Education in any fair trade
Is worth the efforts made.
Do not doubt whatsoever;
Stay bright, hard-working and clever.
Thursday 04.02.2021

February 18

If you come across
A person who is cross
Without any good reason,
Keep calm at any season.

Thursday 04.02.2021

February 19

A victory in an argument, friend,
Comes easy and with a dividend,
Here is how:
Avoid it here and now.

Thursday 04.02.2021

February 20

A GREATful person is the one
Who is able to thank
Whether s/he has lost or won;
Is organized, gentle and frank.

Thursday 04.02.2021

February 21

Smart people contemplate
What is on their plate
And how much for health's sake.
In cuisine and work, pick up your "bake".
Thursday 04.02.2021

February 22

Courage is of essence in all:
Cooking, research, work, playing ball.
Be courageous and wise;
Remain gentle; be clever; prioritize.
Thursday 04.02.2021

February 23

Emotions are spice:
Use them with measure –
No need to be like ice; –
Just stay in control of this treasure.
Thursday 04.02.2021

February 24

Tired people, indeed,
Produce corresponding results as a rule,
Whether giving a speech or taking the lead.
Be smart to refuel.

Sunday 07.02.2021

February 25

Order in art
Is a huge part.
Observe to excel;
Create, get on well.

Sunday 07.02.2021

February 26

Keep plain your discourse,
Whether you write or present.
Let your speech be gentle, not coarse.
Audience and context help pick the extent.

Sunday 07.02.2021

February 27

All things are good in due course.
Be not sorry, but thankful, of course.
In autumn: harvest and mow –
For in winter it is going to snow.

Sunday 07.02.2021

February 28

God gave us not the spirit of fear,
But of power, love and of a sound mind.
Therefore, keep your outlook clear;
Keep all worries behind.

* See also 2Tim. 1:8.

Sunday 07.02.2021

February 29

A little place for wonder
Is what we need in thunder.
Let your faith become a guide;
Rough weather or calm, let it never slide.

Sunday 07.02.2021

SPRING

March 1

If you present or speak,
Let oxygen and rest
Be your helpful mates to give you zest;
Let them help you breathe and do your best.
Sunday 07.02.2021

March 2

A new day is a new chance to succeed.
Pray and plan and with caution proceed.
Let your business thrive;
Let your project go successfully live.
Sunday 07.02.2021

March 3

Guard your heart
In all you do –
Working, studying, pushing a shopping cart –
To complete your tasks all the way through.
Thursday – Saturday 25–27.02.2021

March 4

Your family, man,
Loves you and has a plan
To help you succeed:
In all good things – make sure you heed.
Thursday 25.02.2021

March 5

In every situation
The Lord is with you.
Remember; forsake hesitation.
He makes your victories great and your troubles few.
Thursday 25.02.2021

March 6

Never grow to forsake
Your kind dreams,
Whatever persistent efforts they take;
However distant the victory seems.
Thursday – Friday 25–26.02.2021

March 7

Trust God in all –
This includes studies and work –
This is the Christ's call,
Do not worry whether you live in Peg or New York.
Friday 26.02.2021

March 8

In sports and studies;
With family and buddies;
In things big and small; in deed and in word,
Praise the Lord!
Friday 26.02.2021

March 9

If wisdom or patience are the things you lack;
If anything else is in low supply,
Do not worry, do not cry, –
Ask God Who gives for free and asks not back.
Friday 26.02.2021

March 10

The worst thing you can do is despair –
Believe, God is Strong to repair.
However bad or irreplaceable it may seem –
He is the One Who can restore and make it gleam.
Friday 26.02.2021

March 11

However hard your work is,
Remember about cheer,
Whether you go far or near,
Whether you are a doc or in biz…
Saturday 27.02.2021

March 12

Do the right thing
And God will do the rest:
Whatever life situations bring –
He will bless to do your best.
Sunday 07.03.2021

March 13

Do not be afraid of changes
When the situation rearranges.
Be consistent in good deeds, pray.
May the Lord bless your every new day.
Sunday 07.03.2021

March 14

Look around:
The sun, your family, the creek sound,
Your every body member...
Wherever you journey, be thankful, remember.
Sunday 07.03.2021

March 15

The Lord our God is the Friend
Who will never depart
From the beginning until the end;
He is the One to Whom you can open your heart.
Sunday 07.03.2021

March 16

Have you ever thought of leisure
As if it were precious treasure?
Spend it wisely to get things done and amaze.
Too much of it, though, is known as laze.

Sunday 07.03.2021

March 17

A wise person thinks
Before shooting a reply.
With haste, errors happen as an eye winks.
Be swift to think and be a smart guy.

Sunday 07.03.2021

March 18

Confidence is what we prefer, –
No need to dismiss doubt.
Just try to address questions, not to defer;
Let your decision-making be stout.

Sunday 07.03.2021

March 19

Christianity is the way of life,
Whether you are with your husband or wife,
At work or at school,
Do not worry, stay cool.

Sunday 07.03.2021

March 20

If you leave your job,
Do so on a positive note;
No need to praise it all or sob
As you may need to return to the boat.

March 2021

March 21

When you hear
Good or critical words,
Some of them may be fair and dear,
But some are just verbal swords.

Thursday 11.03.2021

March 22

If of others you demand a lot,
You should likewise
Demand of yourself regarding all the things you wrought.
So, embrace the Golden Rule and realize.

Thursday 11.03.2021

March 23

The truth is important in all,
But it should be coupled with charity to support.
Charity is important in order not to hurt,
But it should be coupled with the the truth to stand and not to fall.

Thursday 11.03.2021

March 24

A generous sower
Will be a generous mower.
We never know
What will wither, what will grow.

Thursday 11.03.2021

March 25

When we give, let us do so
With the heart full of cheer.
For those who thus bestow
Please the Lord and have their mind clear.
Thursday 11.03.2021

March 26

Not by force and rage,
But by faith and cheer
Christians engage
And win, and advance their career.
Saturday 13.03.2021

March 27

One act of kindness can go
A long way changing the present
Of a rich man and a poor peasant,
Mending things and helping the future's flow.
Sunday 21.03.2021

March 28

It is natural to doubt
For a wise person, eh.
To help figure out:
Worry not, reflect and pray.
Sunday 21.03.2021

March 29

Treat your spouse with respect.
No need to neglect
Simple deeds of kindness and words of support,
Laughing together, doing sport.
Sunday 21.03.2021

March 30

If someone makes a mistake, –
Be careful in order not to lie and take
The stuff upon yourself to cover
A boss, a friend, a music lover…
Sunday 21.03.2021

March 31

Who wouldn't like
To change this world at least a bit
Making it a place for love a better fit?
A kind deed at a time, no need for a loud mike…
Sunday 21.03.2021

April 1

If you are right,
Do not pretend that you are not;
However, to avoid an unnecessary fight
Consider agreeing to differ, stick to light.
Sunday 21.03.2021

April 2

Before you challenge,
It is wise to double-check from the start
All the facts before any damage is done.
In many cases you may find to be in the wrong, at least in part.
Sunday 21.03.2021

April 3

Have you ever seen
The video of the iguana escaping snakes?
Think – what could have been…
Be like the iguana; be active and avoid stepping on rakes.
Sunday 21.03.2021

April 4

Haste makes waste –
These words are wise:
Sometimes they lost who raced.
Be steady avoiding delays though; plan, pray, realize.
Sunday 21.03.2021

April 5

There is a lot of trouble for just men,
But the Lord delivers them out of all.
A troublemaker stumbles and falls then,
But the eyes of the Lord are on the just to hear their every call.
Sunday 28.03.2021

April 6

Never have I seen
A righteous person without help
Or his/her posterity lack bread or yelp –
The opposite situation with the wicker has been.
Thursday 01.04.2021

April 7

Keep silence before the Lord always;
Do not get irritated
Against people who made crooked their ways.
Trust in the Lord however long you may have waited.
Thursday 01.04.2021

April 8

All evildoers and one
Are going to be rooted out,
No matter how much they have won;
There will be no one to help however much they shout.
Thursday 01.04.2021

April 9

A little more
And nothing will be found
Of those who unleash war,
Who discern not where they are bound.
Thursday 01.04.2021

April 10

The Lord laughs at evildoers, indeed.
He sees that their day approaches for their deed.
The Lord's eyes are upon the righteous, truly,
To save and to deliver them fully.
Thursday 01.04.2021

April 11

Few things of a poor man
Are better than riches of a wicked one.
The inheritance of the just stays with their own clan; –
Acquisitions of the unrighteous come and are gone.
Thursday 01.04.2021

April 12

It often happens with support
That it comes from places least expected
In studies and work, in life and sport
Praise the Lord Who blessed your way to be perfected.
Thursday 01.04.2021

April 13

Strengthen your hearts,
All who trust in the Lord truly day and night:
His Love for His people never departs;
Even if they fall, He will make them see the light.
Thursday 01.04.2021

April 14

As Kipling noted:
The strength of the pack is the wolf, indeed;
And the strength of the wolf is the pack to protect and to feed.
Reflect on this concept quoted.
Sunday 04.04.2021

April 15

I hoped in the Lord and acted:
He delivered me and protected.
Glory be to my Saviour now and forever!
Let my lips pronounce praise, let me be truly clever.
Sunday 04.04.2021

April 16

I will praise the Lord wherever I go.
He is my Deliverer; out of all He saved and made me glow.
Trust in God however harsh it is –
He makes burning darts vanish and sends a pleasant breeze.
Sunday 04.04.2021

April 17

All truly smart people are believers;
They are faith, hope and love receivers.
If you are smart, believe;
May the Lord help you with all good things to receive.
Friday 09.04.2021

April 18

Never get despaired.
Whatever you worry about, it can be repaired.
Believe in God and do your part –
May He rejoice and strengthen your heart.
Friday 09.04.2021

April 19

However busy it gets,
Remember the Lord and the poor.
Remember to smile whatever upsets.
Shine, win, endure.
Friday 09.04.2021

April 20

Remember how you moved to a new place;
How you coped with all the tasks at an incredible pace;
How you were hungry and fed a poor guy?
To all who think you lack courage, say goodbye.
Sunday 18.04.2021

April 21

Believe, friend:
Miracles happen, God works them all the time.
Just hope, whatever is the trend.
Keep going and pray to turn into juice your lime.

Sunday 18.04.2021

April 22

Do not despise
Small acts of kindness whatever is the day.
Practise, thank others for them and awesomize;
Think big, be wise and pray.

Sunday 18.04.2021

April 23

Do not rush with your decision,
Especially at work with a colleague –
Explore any matter with precision;
Attain the highest league.

Thursday 22.04.2021

April 24

Don't be afraid –
Rely on God in all good deeds:
He is the One Who protects and feeds,
Who heard you whenever you prayed.
Friday 23.04.2021

April 25

Faith is seen in deeds.
Words without kind acts
Are like useless weeds,
Like constant calling that distracts.
Friday 23.04.2021

April 26

Whatever is the situation,
Deploy your faith and wit
With sober, true examination;
Add a pinch of courage to the kit.
Friday 23.04.2021

April 27

Let your heart not feel lonely.
There is one thing to remember only:
You love God and God loves you.
Cheer up; faith, hope and love will help break through.
Friday 23.04.2021

April 28

If you are a team leader,
You are not a boss, you are a feeder.
Take good care:
Keep order; support; help glare.
Tuesday 27.04.2021

April 29

Think if you need to complain –
Not all things are proper
And not all on a plane.
May the Lord make you a coper.
Tuesday 27.04.2021

April 30

The just rejoice in the Lord alway.
He shows them solutions and the true Way;
He is their armour against worry.
In Him the righteous glory.
See also Ps. 64.
Tuesday 27.04.2021

May 1

Let the heart
Of those who seek the Lord rejoice:
The Lord is with you to bless your start,
To help with your choice.
See also Ps. 69.
Friday 30.04.2021

May 2

To avoid disappointment in things
Consider what it is that brings
It about;
Be faithful, loving and stout.
Saturday 01.05.2021

May 3

No one needs love that's blind, –
Sometimes it is a good thing to use your mind.
Love does need to be true,
And also it needs to be wise to break through.
Saturday 01.05.2021

May 4

If you are hired,
Do well, no need to overdo.
If for whatever unworthy reason you are fired,
Pray, search, be steady – you will break through.
Monday 03.05.2021

May 5

However busy,
Stick to prayer –
This makes things easy
And successful for a teacher and a mayor.
Monday 03.05.2021

May 6

Support your family, man,
In sport, work, studies to plan
And succeed,
As much as they need.
Monday 03.05.2021

May 7

Do not harden your heart,
Whether you succeed or fail.
Stay humane in full, not in part,
Regardless of what they mix in their cocktail.
Monday 03.05.2021

May 8

Technology is not bad
When it works, lad,
But it often does not –
Be realistic, plan a lot.
Monday 03.05.2021

May 9

Some things when arrive,
Make little to no sense.
Do not be angry, strive, –
A lot of those turn out in your defence.
Monday 03.05.2021

May 10

Which prayer is best?
No, this ain't a test.
The one that's long, short or fast?
The one from the heart, the one that does last.
Monday 03.05.2021

May 11

If a job is in the way
Of prayer –
Change something straight away;
Listen not to a naysayer.
Monday 03.05.2021

May 12

All lives matter,
No exception,
No clatter:
People, animals, plants – a true conception.
Thursday – Friday 06–07.05.2021

May 13

If you ever fall back,
Make sure that faith is not what you lack;
Yet better, fall forward, friend –
That way you'll see what to amend.
Saturday 08.05.2021

May 14

When you work and fail,
That is a result,
Just as Edison had on his trail.
Laziness, passiveness and undecidedness are an achievement
insult.
Saturday 08.05.2021

May 15

Faithful people should never worry –
They are never left by themselves, to the Lord's glory.
Therefore, if you do well and fail, do not be sorry –
Work on, better stuff is on its way for your story.
Saturday 08.05.2021

May 16

Years are like small grains in a sand clock.
Waste them not,
Smile a lot.
The Lord loves and cares for His flock.
Saturday 08.05.2021

May 17

How to conquer worry
Before it conquers you?
One kind deed daily to God's glory;
Pray, work, rest, enjoy morning dew.
Tuesday 11.05.2021

May 18

God has not given us any kind
Of the spirit of fear, –
But of power, love and of a sound mind –
Remember, you'll go far, you won't go near.
    * *See also 2Tim. 1:7.*
                        Tuesday 11.05.2021

May 19

Communication with family
Is the way to be strong and wise
For any Jo and Emily;
Stick together, visit, phone, email, awesomize.
                        Tuesday 11.05.2021

May 20

Do not take lightly
God's commandments, friend.
Do not overdo, just do it rightly;
Love, have faith through deeds, amend.
                        Tuesday 11.05.2021

May 21

Oh, how important is your clan!
Although it may be tough with your family, man,
But stick together and so educate
Your children; prosper, stay strong, navigate.
Tuesday 11.05.2021

May 22

When times are tough,
When some do laugh –
Remember, the Lord is with you now and forever.
Do your work, let criticism go, be clever.
Tuesday 11.05.2021

May 23

Right decisions, truly,
Lead to right ones later too.
Be wise, those pay back fully;
One right decision at a time to break through…
Tuesday 11.05.2021

May 24

Sport is a factor in health
To keep all out of worry, closer to wealth;
To rest from sedentary work;
To stay away from a cork.

Saturday 22.05.2021

May 25

Einstein, Caruso, Dickens, Ma, Wells –
Some of the names whose work sells,
But also the ones who were heavily criticised.
Despite all they withstood and realised.

Sunday 23.05.2021

May 26

"He That sent Me is with Me: the Father has not left Me
alone."*
You, too, remember –
January through December –
When you meet face to face, online, on the phone…

    * See Jn. 8:29.

Sunday 23.05.2021

May 27

If in doubt , try –
You may succeed.
Sometimes it does not pay to be shy –
Be wise, courageous, lead.

Sunday 23.05.2021

May 28

Fill your thought
With courage truly –
This is what Carnegie taught
To eliminate worry and to live fully.

Sunday 23.05.2021

May 29

Thank God for all with heart sincere:
Your health, looks, wisdom, food, life, children, spouse…
May He make your mind clear
And direct you to more good things through which to thankfully
browse.

Sunday 23.05.2021

May 30

The righteous bring fruit that's good
Even in their old age.
What to say to conclude?
With such fill your stage.
See also Ps. 92.
Sunday 23.05.2021

May 31

Think of your enemies no more,
Neither good nor bad,
In order not to give them power over you on the floor;
In order to be sound and healthy, lad.
Sunday 23.05.2021

SUMMER

June 1

The righteous ought to rejoice;
The Lord has helped them make the right choice.
The Lord reigns!
Light for the pure-hearted always remains.
Sunday 30.05.2021

June 2

The strength of the strongest
Is to never despair,
Even if their wait is the longest
And to be wise and patient to repair.
Tuesday 01.06.2021

June 3

Sometimes it is better to speak less
Unless you want to confess
To the lack of your knowledge and also because
Otherwise you may seem rude without any good cause.
Wednesday 02.06.2021

June 4

Avoid doubt
In work, studies and all;
Apply your efforts to find out
And make decisions that are stout.

Thursday 03.06.2021

June 5

Don't work too hard
To be healthy and of good cheer.
Do work enough and be on guard –
Just have measure and keep your mind clear.

Friday 04.06.2021

June 6

Praise the Lord with heart sincere!
He's made you go far, not near.
Praise Him for His Love pertains.
Wherever you go, with you His Love remains.

Saturday 05.06.2021

June 7

When you get angry, friend,
Contain yourself and have compassion.
None of us is perfect in the end;
Focus on light, life, love, artistic passion.
Saturday 05.06.2021

June 8

Even if you are in a mask
Or on the phone:
Smile to cope with any task
And not to be alone!
Monday 07.06.2021

June 9

God helps not only when all
Is well, but alway;
Therefore, whether you stay or fall,
Don't worry, believe, smile, pray.
Tuesday 08.06.2021

June 10

Don't panic, buddy,
Even when projects are muddy.
Keep calm and work on –
Build your success and confidence thereon.
Wednesday 09.06.2021

June 11

Be like a proton, bud:
Stay positive in all,
Whether you live in Adamstown or Baghdad;
In winter, spring, summer and fall.
Thursday 10.06.2021

June 12

Believe despite all odds,
On a project and when you fish with rods.
This is how Christians differ;
Make your work lighter, not stiffer.
Friday 11.06.2021

June 13

Some rushing after big money
Forget that sweet is honey;
That we only have one life and live today;
That we should do kind things, rest and play.

Saturday 12.06.2021

June 14

The day of rest
Is for man and not the other way around.
When you can take a break go ahead, do your best –
Just do not turn your blind eye on your neighbour's SOS sound.

* See Mk. 2:27.

Sunday 13.06.2021

June 15

Praise the Lord for all!
He hears the poor man's, orphan's, widow's call;
Defends the country's border;
And amongst a storm He establishes order.

Sunday 13.06.2021

June 16

Communication and charity
Are pleasing to God truly
And are required for health and clarity;
Therefore, practise these duly.
      See Heb. 13:16.
          Tuesday 15.06.2021

June 17

God is my Helper – I will not fear
What man shall do unto me.
The Lord has made it clear.
Praise the Lord – He makes us free.
      See Heb. 13:6.
          Wednesday 16.06.2021

June 18

I will never leave
Nor forsake you, –
The Lord reminded to us to believe
And to stick to a courageous, positive view.
      See Heb. 13:5.
          Thursday 17.06.2021

June 19

Praise the Lord,
Jesus Christ the Word!
Triumph and salvation
Are in the house of the just in any nation.

Friday 18.06.2021

June 20

God gave us communication
As a precious gift, indeed.
Use it on projects to succeed;
Use it with clarity, wisdom and admiration.

Saturday 19.06.2021

June 21

It is good to learn from others,
But it is also good to appreciate
Your own stuff among your sisters and brothers;
Be smart and stay up to date.

Sunday 20.06.2021

June 22

Life is worth living, man.
If not for yourself, then
For the Lord and others, indeed,
With faith, hope and love; in word and in deed.
Sunday 20.06.2021

June 23

If you have stumbled
Or meaninglessly mumbled,
Do not worry and do not be sorry.
Stay agile and smile!
Sunday 20.06.2021

June 24

Rest. You need it to work with zest.
To score your goal and to perform best.
It does not have to be a lot, –
Just sleep, relax and practise as often as not.
Sunday 20.06.2021

June 25

In work, studies, life
You may find a real strife
Of someone trying to improve their cheap reputation at your
expense –
Be your own beautiful, courageous, smart self in your defence.
Wednesday 23.06.2021

June 26

If you are an instructor that's smart,
Make building up on strengths a part
Of your every day;
Help your students achieve without delay.
Wednesday 23.06.2021

June 27

If you are a student, mate, –
Learn, but do not change
All the good things you've acquired of late;
Use learning to grow your knowledge range.
Wednesday 23.06.2021

June 28

Worry not,
However hot
Things get –
God will never forget.

Friday 25.06.2021

June 29

If you want more light
In the world around,
Let your own sight be bright,
Let cheerful and faithful be your sound!

Wednesday 23.06.2021

June 30

Blessed are those who fear the Lord,
Who believe and stick to His Word.
They are like a tree beside a river;
Safeguarded by the Lord and His angels who always deliver.

Tuesday 29.06.2021

July 1

Be courageous, friend,
Along with faith, hope, love they lend
To many victories in all
Good things, including ball.

Friday 25.06.2021

July 2

However busy, do not forget ever
That the Lord is with you
To protect and react and to never let
You down, to go with you anew.

Friday 25.06.2021

July 3

Language is a gift –
Use it to help lift
Heavy tasks and to uplift,
But before you say – sift.

Friday 02.07.2021

July 4

Remember to use some joy,
However hard you proceed;
Whether you've achieved a lot or little – enjoy;
Even if you fail today, you will succeed.

Saturday 03.07.2021

July 5

Show respect, appreciate,
Whoever you are:
A teacher, a student, a chief of a state,
A husband, a wife … Both of you will go far.

Wednesday 23.06.2021

July 6

This is a tale
About naysayers:
They usually drink their own cocktail
And before they get to the core, they go through their own
limitation layers.

Friday 25.06.2021

July 7

Live now,
Do good – make it "wow";
Respect, appreciate and do it today;
Till the sun shines make your hay.

Saturday 03.07.2021

July 8

The whole new world is each new day.
If you are not sure where to go – pray;
Let the Lord help you in every worthy endeavour,
With Him you'll never say "never".

Saturday 03.07.2021

July 9

Put your hope in the Lord now and alway:
He'll make you go far or stay,
But either way
It will be to your benefit at the end of the day.

Saturday 03.07.2021

July 10

Sometimes it takes effort, indeed,
To stay positive in everyday feat,
But the Lord helps in every good deed.
Stay positive and let your business be neat.
Friday 09.07.2021

July 11

Don't worry and don't doubt.
The Lord is Strong to make your walk stout.
So, rely on Him in all
And do your part, but do not stall.
Friday 09.07.2021

July 12

At work and home,
In Ottawa and in Rome
Watch the words you say –
Let those shine and not extinguish the way.
Sunday 11.07.2021

July 13

All things are in vain
If the Lord is not with you.
Therefore, what's priority and what is main
Is to seek the Lord each day anew.

Monday 12.07.2021

July 14

Life is to be lived, adhere:
Do work, but rest;
Relax, but conquer fear;
Create good things with zest!

Monday 12.07.2021

July 15

Order in things
Improves business and all.
Use it to enjoy the fruit it brings
And to climb over any wall.

Wednesday 14.07.2021

July 16

The Lord is close to all
Who call on Him with a heart sincere;
Keep believing – do not drop the ball.
Keep your heart and mind clear.
                    Thursday 15.07.2021

July 17

The situation around may rapidly change,
And some things are impossible to expect,
But you believe whatever the range,
Be calm and wise to react.
                    Friday 16.07.2021

July 18

Sometimes it is better to make a mistake
Than to be indecisive, indeed.
For some decisions are correct for you to take,
And others can be amended if you carefully proceed.
                    Saturday 17.07.2021

July 19

The Lord is the Wind in my sail,
From rooftops I am proclaiming;
He is my Support when I win or fail –
With Him all issues I am taming.

Sunday 18.07.2021

July 20

Remember to sincerely smile,
Even if you are on the phone:
This is to help hone
Soft skills and to stay agile.

Monday 19.07.2021

July 21

Praise the Lord with all,
In your work and leisure,
In a park and mall.
He is our only True Treasure!

Tuesday 20.07.2021

July 22

Do things with love.
It does not matter what others do –
You do right to earn a peace dove
And to break through.

Wednesday 21.07.2021

July 23

Let wisdom guide;
Let care abide;
Be your true, smart self, remain kind;
Let anger, sadness or joy never make you blind.

Wednesday 21.07.2021

July 24

Rely on God with all your heart
And do not rely on your smartness alone
In work, studies and art;
In person, online, on the phone…

Friday 23.07.2021

July 25

Do not be wise
In your own eyes.
Turn away from stuff that's bad –
Do not listen to that cunning lad.

Saturday 24.07.2021

July 26

Honour the Lord with all your possession
And with all your earnings truly.
He will protect you in any recession
And will make your garden bloom fully.

* See Pr. 3:9-10.

Sunday 25.07.2021

July 27

Loving parents correct
Their child and do not neglect.
When the Lord sends you a trial,
Reflect, pray, thank, be agile.

Sunday 25.07.2021

July 28

If you have shopping or another passion,
Stay in control of this art
For successful progression –
Let nothing possess your heart.
Tuesday 27.07.2021

July 29

Those who look for wisdom, find,
But those who have something else in mind
Risk losing it all.
Love wisdom to prosper and not to fall.
Wednesday 28.07.2021

July 30

Listen to people to learn,
Including to those who do not speak much,
Whether they speak plain English or Dutch.
You do not have to adhere, but do discern.
Thursday 29.07.2021

July 31

Rely on God in all,
Including work and studies;
Do not drop the ball,
Amongst strangers or buddies.
                              Friday 30.07.2021

August 1

Riches do not save in the day of distress,
But justice in the heart and actions does.
Adjust your ways more, stock up less;
Discern what's right, what's buzz.
                              Saturday 31.07.2021

August 2

Happy is he who is wise:
He has a long life, is rich and health is his prize.
The beginning of wisdom is to fear God rightly
To glorify Him, to love, to think, speak and act brightly.
                              Saturday 31.07.2021

August 3

Your family wants you to succeed,
To be happy, to lead.
Therefore, consider their advice;
Be wise; if you disagree, be nice.

Monday 02.08.2021

August 4

Don't delay to donate
If you are able to;
Do not over-contemplate
For both of you to get through.

Tuesday 03.08.2021

August 5

Do not reflect about bad stuff for your neighbour
Without any reason truly –
Focus on your studies and labour,
Let God deal with the things they do fully.

Tuesday 03.08.2021

August 6

Citius, altius, fortius* is the way to go
In studies, work and all:
Keep going, row.
If you hit it, climb over the wall.
* Latin for "faster, higher, stronger".
Thursday 05.08.2021

August 7

Arrogance precedes a fall –
Humbleness lends to success.
What to choose is your call.
Believe more, worry less.
Friday 06.08.2021

August 8

It is better to have less
And be in peace
Than to have lots with a mess.
Be thankful and if you worry, cease.
* See Pr. 15:16-17; 17:1.
Saturday 07.08.2021

August 9

He who can master
Himself before getting angry or upset
Is likely to be healthy and earn a dime faster
Than the one who is rich, but tends to fret.
Saturday 07.08.2021

August 10

An impulsive idea
Is not always great.
Whether you go far or near,
Weigh all things to go or to wait.
Monday 09.08.2021

August 11

Be not only a listener or sayer,
But a doer in all good things:
Faith, hope, love, prayer…
Regardless of your "year rings".
Tuesday 10.08.2021

August 12

Rely on God when you wake and go to bed;
When all is good and when times are tough –
He protects the righteous and the wicked fall instead.
Be loving, faithful, courageous and gentle, but never rough.
Wednesday 11.08.2021

August 13

No reason is needed
For good deeds to be seeded,
For a smile or laughter sincere –
Be your kind self, smart and with good cheer!
Wednesday 11.08.2021

August 14

When things take place,
Address them at a reasonable pace –
Do not freak out or be upset.
Be wise and patient, do not regret.
Wednesday 11.08.2021

August 15

Love is all the words you say,
All the deeds,
The things for which you pray.
Therefore, plant worthy seeds.

Friday 13.08.2021

August 16

It often happens so
That your elder family members
Know better where and how to go,
Because they have more experience and do remember.

Sunday 15.08.2021

August 17

If you are in doubt, pray –
May the Lord direct your steps;
Remember also what they say:
Wins he who preps.

Monday 16.08.2021

August 18

Love nature, friend!
What for to wait for leaders' visions
Or big political decisions?
Do what matters in the end.

Monday 16.08.2021

August 19

The Lord has not given to us
The spirit of worry,
But of faith, hope and love in stock
To our benefit and to His glory.

Tuesday 17.08.2021

August 20

Colleague, do not worry
As this does not help your story –
Have patience and faith instead,
Whether you pronounce it [zi:] or [zed].

Tuesday 19.08.2021

August 21

Be wise and keep it simple truly
To get your reward duly,
To succeed in every enterprise
And to win a worthy prize.

Tuesday 17.08.12.2021

August 22

Keep hope
And make right decisions today.
Be strong to say "nope";
Be tough to work and smart to play.

Friday 20.08.2021

August 23

There are many things around –
You have to choose
What is vane and what is sound
In order to win and not to lose.

Tuesday 17.08.2021

August 24

There is a difference, indeed,
Between loving chocolate and someone;
Make sure you discern to rightly proceed
And to say "I have won".
Tuesday 17.08.2021

August 25

What if you know
More than your instructor
And on experience you are not low?
Do not worry, but find a way to grow.
Tuesday 17.08.2021

August 26

The ability to stay in control
Of your feelings is a crown
With which wise rulers roll.
Learn where to stay cool and where to frown.
Tuesday 17.08.2021

August 27

Do not trust all –
Listen to the wise.
At home, at work, with buddies, in a mall...
Make sure that caution is something you exercise.
Tuesday 17.08.2021

August 28

Whatever you do,
Make it to God's glory;
Be wise, kind and faithful all the way through,
Whether you wear a white collar or drive a lorry.
Wednesday 25.08.2021

August 29

It is better to be patient, indeed,
Than to be quarrelsome and to vainly plead.
Believe to find your way,
Regardless of what rejectors say.
Saturday 28.08.2021

August 30

When all things are well,
Enjoy and thank.
When things do not sell –
Reflect, be frank.

Saturday 28.08.2021

August 31

Be neither righteous too much
Nor overly wise
Because things as such
Cause peril and unnecessary bitter cries.

Saturday 28.08.2021

AUTUMN

September 1

Don't be unrighteous to an extent extreme
Or unwise without a ray of light.
Why to be punished or be obliged to leave your team?
Keep healthy altruism in sight.

Saturday 28.08.2021

September 2

Do not rush to show your anger, man,
If you do not want to be put under a ban
By your subordinates, boss or peer.
Be wise and work with cheer.

Saturday 28.08.2021

September 3

Work that's steady
Makes your path to success ready.
Start in the morning in fifth gear
And work with cheer.

Sunday 29.08.2021

September 4

Retribution comes for all,
Be it in hundred years, in ten or now.
One reaps based on how one does plough.
Be smart, thrive, avoid a fall.

Sunday 29.08.2021

September 5

Have you ever heard "repent"?
That thing is not to make resent,
But to change the course and to appease;
To fill your sail with a breeze.

Sunday 29.08.2021

September 6

Those who love good do well,
But good also needs protection
Against confusion and deception.
Do not hide your talents in a void cell.

Sunday 29.08.2021

September 7

Don't let yourself be lazy
In prayer, studies, work and sport:
Don't do anything crazy;
With one brick at a time build your fort.
Monday 06.09.2021

September 8

Guard your heart,
From it come all things:
A happy ending and a successful start;
Confidence and wide spread wings…
Tuesday 07.09.2021

September 9

There is a measure
In all: work, studies, rest;
Sorrow, sleep, leisure…
Those who use it have found a treasure.
Wednesday 08.09.2021

September 10

No one is perfect in all,
That is why diversity is what we need, –
But not in everything, indeed,
Only in good, Christian things to stand tall.

Thursday 09.09.2021

September 11

It may not sound humble
When people do mumble
About their good deeds,
But let mimicking good stuff be to what it leads.

Friday 10.09.2021

September 12

When you can do good, do,
When help is needed:
It will help, you too, get through,
And many good examples will be seeded.

Friday 10.09.2021

September 13

It is good to glorify the Lord,
To sing to Him and to praise
In deed, thought and word;
In work, studies and rest without laze.
Sunday 12.09.2021

September 14

One good deed and decision
Trigger others, like a ripple;
And wrong ones, similarly acting, may cripple.
Ask the Lord to help you clear your vision.
Monday 13.09.2021

September 15

Never lose hope
As the Lord is Strong to make you cope,
To support anyone on a slope
And to give wisdom to communicate "nope".
Tuesday 14.09.2021

September 16

The environment is the home
And we are to improve and take care,
Wherever we roam:
Sea, space, earth and air…

Wednesday 15.09.2021

September 17

Let your prayers,
Let your deeds be sincere.
He wins who dares!
Read, run, gear.

Thursday 16.09.2021

September 18

Health is important, for sure.
Take good care, heed.
In the sea and ashore,
Even when some mislead.

Friday 17.09.2021

September 19

To give up and not to try
Is easy, for sure,
But to have wisdom and faith to fly
Is what takes a bit more.

Saturday 18.09.2021

September 20

Persistence is the tool
Of those who have obtained a PhD.
So, use it in all things that are cool,
Whether you live around the Dnipro or the Dee.

Sunday 19.09.2021

September 21

Pray on whatsoever,
Whether things are smooth or tough,
Thank the Lord ever;
May He make you cheerfully laugh.

Monday 20.09.2021

September 22

Have space for joy
In your schedule alway.
Sing, cook, play...
Be of good cheer, shine your way.

Monday 20.09.2021

September 23

The Golden Rule* is about
Treating others as you want to be treated.
So, regardless of all, do stand out –
Let your gentle, kind style be never depleted.

* See Mt. 7:12; Lk. 6:31.

Wednesday 22.09.2021

September 24

Learn God's ways
And share them with others.
Let the Lord bless all your days;
Let your lips be filled with praise!

Thursday 23.09.2021

September 25

Friday evenings are for rest
And to take care of your "nest";
To do your own stuff or go to a fest
And to share with your family your best.
Friday 24.09.2021

September 26

It is never too late
To repent and to fix,
Regardless of the state –
Just start putting right those bricks.
Saturday 25.09.2021

September 27

With a prayer in the morning and in the eve;
With it I come, and with it I leave;
It helps make a decision;
And in studies and work it increases precision.
Sunday 26.09.2021

September 28

Be gentle whatsoever;
Be kind and clever;
Do not imitate negative stuff, –
Let your heart and mind be solid – not fluff.
Sunday 01.12.2013

September 29

Keep your chin up and smile, –
It does not have to be big,
Just have faith and be agile;
Direct wisely your brig.
Tuesday 28.09.2021

September 30

In every situation be wise
In order not to lose, but to win a prize.
Let your style be light,
Let your ideas be bright.
Tuesday 29.09.2021

October 1

In work and studies choose order to pursue –
This should help your steady advance,
At least it helped the famous few.
Rely on it, don't take a chance.

Tuesday 28.09.2021

October 2

A plan without haste;
A life that's courageous and chaste;
A way full of faith, love and hope
Are the things to withstand any slope.

Tuesday 28.09.2021

October 3

Sometimes gratitude
Is what defines person's altitude,
Their sincerity and attitude,
Their charm and aptitude.

Thursday 30.09.2021

October 4

Things make sense when you live by the Book*.
You can always check it when unsure
To ensure positivity of your outlook;
To align with faith, hope and love as if a ship with the shore.
     * *The Bible.*
Thursday 30.09.2021

October 5

Can one become a hero right now and here?
Yes, but that is rare.
More often than not
Heroes are those who steadily give all that they've got.
Saturday 02.10.2021

October 6

Being evil is hard
On your brain, liver, lungs and heart.
In contrast, being kind
Is healthy keeping sound your mind.
Saturday 02.10.2021

October 7

Being popular in fame
Sometimes makes people lame.
They depend on a like or go highbrow
And forget to enjoy simple moments of "wow".
Saturday 02.10.2021

October 8

Sometimes it takes efforts to choose
Between wrong and right;
And since it is easy to lose,
Ask the Lord to always lead you to light.
Saturday 02.10.2021

October 9

If you would like
To please all,
You are on a flat tire bike.
Stop, do right before you fall.
Saturday 02.10.2021

October 10

Do not expect all
To wish to teach you to fish.
If you don't want to stall,
Work on to fill with knowledge your dish.

Saturday 02.10.2021

October 11

Speaking without listening through
Is like touching hot glue,
Like using a compass that is not true.
Be patient, avoid hurry that is undue.

Sunday 10.10.2021

October 12

If you haven't been to the Church for some time,
Try, it is like a vacation:
Your mind switches from worries and dime;
For soul and heart, it is relaxation.

Sunday 10.10.2021

October 13

Not all right things are hard;
Not all good things cost much.
So, pray and be on guard;
Use your head and heart.
Sunday 10.10.2021

October 14

If you work with a person who is sly,
Do not be afraid, neither be shy,
Especially avoid worry –
The Lord is Strong to make you shine in glory.
Sunday 10.10.2021

October 15

The just one,
Even though trapped, escapes,
And the wicked person takes his place.
Moreover, the just has won the race.
Sunday 10.10.2021

October 16

It is good to live separately, but close
To your family, man.
They help and support you against any foes, –
Yet, no one gets tired of the clan.
Monday 11.10.2021

October 17

Pay attention to your way,
Do not go astray
Left or right;
Have faith and pray.
See also Pr. 4:26-27.
Monday 11.10.2021

October 18

Things that are kind and brute
Are in the speaker's power,
So are things that are bitter, sweet and sour.
Whatever one chooses will eat of its fruit.
Monday 11.10.2021

October 19

Person's words
Seem just before the other party speaks,
At which point they start resembling swords.
Be wise to listen – finds he who seeks.
Monday 11.10.2021

October 20

Those who are slow
To anger in word, deed and thought
Extinguish fire and avoid a blow.
Not by it, but by wisdom true victories are brought.
Monday 11.10.2021

October 21

In sadness and joy,
In studies and work,
With family, friends
Have Christ before you despite all trends.
Tuesday 12.10.2021

October 22

When God shows mercy to a man,
Even his enemies look favourably at him,
And success follows every worthy plan.
Pray, believe; avoid whim.
Tuesday 12.10.2021

October 23

Those who possess themselves are better than
Those possessing big riches.
Be gentle, especially with your clan
And make on time your stitches.
Tuesday 12.10.2021

October 24

What makes a good leader?
Big knowledge, charm, communication?
Yes, but above all, a good one is a seeder
Of best things in his team without excessive frustration.
Thursday 14.10.2021

October 25

Have you ever wanted to be a leader?
If so, you've wished well,
But a good one is a team feeder.
Therefore, while you can, enjoy what other positions "sell".
Thursday 14.10.2021

October 26

When you purchase a thing,
Yes, consider your need,
But also the environment, indeed,
And that the Earth has a lot of children to feed.
Thursday 14.10.2021

October 27

According to Carnegie's book*,
Those who can't conquer worry have a sad end.
So, regardless of what they may cook,
Believe and remember that the Lord is your Friend.
* Dale Carnegie's "How to stop worrying and start living".
Thursday 14.10.2021

October 28

Is there any good in retail?
Yes, as it gives necessities and the convenience they entail.
We only need to use it with measure
And to learn to share good stuff with pleasure.
Thursday 14.10.2021

October 29

Love your dog for what it is
And not for what you want it to be:
Your walks and friendship will be a breeze;
You'll learn to be and to set free.
Thursday 14.10.2021

October 30

Happiness is not about having a thing –
It is a state of mind.
Have faith, work, rest, sing,
Pray, be gentle and kind.
Thursday 14.10.2021

October 31

All who work get sticky moments.
Do not lose courage or cheer;
Do your work, whether alone or with a peer;
Make sure your communication is clear.

Thursday 14.10.2021

November 1

Rely on God in all
And do your part.
He is the One Who blesses your start
And makes joyful and strong you heart.

Thursday 14.10.2021

November 2

If you are a team player,
It is a gift to your team,
But discern where to give more (or less) steam
To be a goer and not a stayer.

Thursday 14.10.2021

November 3

Whatever you hear,
Take it with a grain
Of salt, use your brain,
Use your heart to go far, not near.

Thursday 14.10.2021

November 4

There is no situation
Which you cannot make worse.
Therefore, avoid the "burn it all" temptation
And wisely run your course.

Thursday 14.10.2021

November 5

If you work on a project with a client,
Set fair expectations
And remain compliant
For many happy congratulations.

Thursday 14.10.2021

November 6

Do not scrutinize yourself to succeed:
Request enough time,
Avoid greed;
Make juice if you receive a lime.
Thursday 14.10.2021

November 7

There is no other way,
But through Christ, indeed.
Therefore, believe and pray
For every achievement or need.
Thursday 14.10.2021

November 8

Be like a hummingbird:
Beautiful, smart, fast;
Whether you are in construction or an IT nerd;
Savour the present, learn from the past.
Thursday 14.10.2021

November 9

Be the light
In any situation.
Do things, say words which are right;
Be gentle and positive through abundance and deprivation.
Thursday 14.10.2021

November 10

Grow in good stuff,
Though it may be busy and tough;
Let your good deeds now exceed
Those that did precede.
Thursday 14.10.2021

November 11

Plant flowers and trees;
Plant also good deeds
Without worry or charging exceeding fees;
Plant fair, gentle seeds.
Thursday 14.10.2021

November 12

If you tend to freak out,
Calm down.
Have more faith and less doubt;
Smile more, minimize frown.
Thursday 14.10.2021

November 13

You end up with
What you invest in.
So, choose important things, please.
You have the day to seize.
Sunday 17.10.2021

November 14

A faithful wife is a treasure;
Well raised children are a pleasure.
Be faithful and support
Your family rightly, your true and loving cohort.
Thursday 21.10.2021

November 15

When you do a kind deed,
Never be sorry –
Do it to the Lord's glory
And for the sake of your neighbour, indeed.

Thursday 21.10.2021

November 16

Tune your heart to prayer:
It will help you be a mayor;
It will protect your body and mind;
It will help you advance and not fall behind.

Thursday 21.10.2021

November 17

Make the truth your arm and armour.
It leads to the finish line;
It keeps many doors open and fine.
Its value will never decline.

Thursday 21.10.2021

November 18

Love God with all your heart.
Respect your neighbour.
With these two things in life and art
You are going to succeed in your labour.
Thursday 21.10.2021

November 19

Things do not always go
According to your plan.
Thank the Lord for all, though,
For He has been with your wherever you ran.
Thursday 21.10.2021

November 20

Unexpected things do happen each day,
But you do not freak out:
Do what you can: skip, solve, fix and pray;
Other things are not worthy to be worried about.
Thursday 21.10.2021

November 21

Whatever is the situation,
Possess yourself, avoid frustration,
Even when unexpected things arrive.
Learn when to jump and when to dive.
Thursday 21.10.2021

November 22

It is easy to thank
When all is well every day,
But to be grateful and pray
Alway is a Christian call, I can say.
Sunday 24.10.2021

November 23

Jesus is the Truth, the Way
And to trust Him anyway,
Despite all odds, and do our part
Is the Christian thing to have in our heart.
Sunday 24.10.2021

November 24

No pain, no gain;
No bees, no honey,
No work, no money…
Is what the wisdom of generations does explain.
Sunday 24.10.2021

November 25

When you are able to help, do;
Never mind if it seems small –
Sometimes this is what helps break through, –
Only let your heart be true.
Sunday 24.10.2021

November 26

You have a beautiful smile.
Use it – it will help you and others –
Yes, even when you work on a difficult file,
Among young folks and seasoned mothers and fathers.
Sunday 24.10.2021

November 27

A family is the strength of a society, truly,
A union of a woman and a man.
To support families fully
Is, therefore, wise societies' plan.
Sunday 24.10.2021

November 28

Haste makes waste
At work, in studies, leisure.
Therefore, treat time as treasure.
Do not hurry even if it is just "copy and paste".
Monday 25.10.2021

November 29

Smile often, buddy –
It is one of the biggest soft skills;
It is healthier than many pills;
It helps earn more to pay your bills.
Monday 25.10.2021

November 30

When you prepare a presentation,
Need to speak to a client or defend your dissertation,
Make sure that you have some spare information –
To add to your confidence "ration".

Wednesday 27.10.2021

December 1

Sometimes you need to listen to your heart
For choices right,
For a happy end and a successful start.
Let your head and heart make your decisions bright.
Thursday 28.10.2021

December 2

It's hard, I know,
But the victory may be a click away.
Just pray and row.
While the sun shines make hay.
Friday 29.10.2021

December 3

The life is short, so, do not waste:
Do kind things, be kind, say kind words;
In kind things, make haste.
To catch the worm, learn from early birds.
Saturday 30.01.2021

December 4

Life is too short to worry,
What you can, correct and do not be sorry.
May the Lord turn your hardships to glory.
Pray and love, may the Lord bless your story.
Saturday 30.10.2021

December 5

We all have a gift –
A precious talent, indeed.
Be wise and swift,
Use it to God's glory in thought, word and deed.
Sunday 31.10.2021

December 6

St. Nicholas was a man,
But to serve the Lord was his plan.
He is known as a saint bestowing with cheer.
Be like him, help your neighbour far and near.
Sunday 28.11.2021

December 7

Do not envy a violent man
And do not choose his ways.
Wins he who sincerely prays;
Be wise, courageous and kind, as much as you can.
Monday 01.11.2021

December 8

If they persecute, remember:
The Lord despises crooked men,
But He helps the righteous Jan. through December.
Help comes to the righteous, even though they do not know how
and when.
Wednesday 03.11.2021

December 9

The Lord is over all the ways
Of those who fear Him and are wise;
For them He changes back stage talks to praise
And a trap to a prize.
Wednesday 03.11.2021

December 10

Pascha, by some known as Easter,
Is about Christ, resurrection and life eternal,
It is about freedom for every brother and sister;
About faith, hope and love fraternal.

Wednesday–Thursday 03–04.11.2021

December 11

God's blessing is on the dwelling of the just.
They do their work and in God they trust.
God rewards them with success;
They earn more, not less.

Friday 05.11.2021

December 12

In what fast does the Lord take pleasure?
In giving to the poor a bit of your treasure;
In consuming all, even good, things with measure;
In supporting the oppressed and enjoying the azure.

Saturday 06.11.2021

December 13

Communion is important for life, health and all;
Prepare and come, do not stall.
Let the Lord help you on your way.
Shine, continue, pray.

Sunday 07.11.2021

December 14

However unexpected the situation may be,
Remember that the Lord is always with thee.
So, chase out any sort of despair;
Avoid worry; one thing at a time to prepare.

Monday 08.11.2021

December 15

The Lord opposes the arrogant in their ways,
But He shows grace
To the humble all days.
Choose and proceed at a steady, confident pace.

* See Pr. 3:34 (3:37).

Tuesday 09.11.2021

December 16

Take good care of your heart,
From it is the source of life, indeed.
Be wise, patient and humble at the end, in the middle, at the start.
Remember about good humour in every worthy deed.
>   *See Pr. 4:23.*
>   *Wednesday 10.11.2021*

December 17

Eat with pleasure
And drink with measure.
Start and end your day with prayer.
Be wise and joyful at home and at the conveyor.
>   *Thursday 11.11.2021*

December 18

If you work hard,
Enjoy as you have a job to guard.
If you find a better place,
Consider, but be cautious, just in case.
>   *Friday 12.11.2021*

December 19

Nothing is impossible with God.
Believe, do good,
Whether you live in the city or in the wood.
Achieve, stay in the positive mood!
>*See Lk. 1:37.*
>>*Saturday 13.11.2021*

December 20

Humour that's light,
Positive, humble, and appropriate truly
Can make communication and projects bright.
Do not overdo, force it, speed up – just do it right.
>*Sunday 14.11.2021*

December 21

If things do not stick together
In rough or calm weather,
The reason is not always you.
Be objective, take it easy, break through.
>*Monday 15.11.2021*

December 22

Do not depend on other people's opinions too much,
However, be polite.
With common sense and humour – keep in touch.
Let your thoughts, words and deeds radiate light.
Tuesday 16.11.2021

December 23

Donate a smile
To your client, colleague, family, friend –
Show your confident, kind style;
Start a positive trend!
Wednesday 17.11.2021

December 24

A good way to spread cheer
Is to embrace it truly;
Even if it means to make an effort fully,
To keep your mind light and clear.
Thursday 18.11.2021

December 25

By what to measure the success
Of Christmas celebration, indeed?
Vacation, food, guests, dress?
By how much Christ there is in it.

Thursday 18.11.2021

December 26

Christmas does not just go away –
It lives on in our hearts showing the way
To the Light, life, freedom, success.
Rejoice more, fear less.

Thursday 18.11.2021

December 27

Educate your children, team –
Do not get angry, lazy or frustrated –
Not to the extent of someone's whim,
Just do your job. What else to be stated?

Monday 01.11.2021

December 28

We should sincerely praise
St. Mary* for Christmas truly
For being humble and fulfilling God's will fully;
For praying for us all days.
> * St. Mary is also known as Theotokos (Gr.: Θεοτόκος)
> – God-Bearer (Ukr.: Богородиця).
> Friday 03.12.2021

December 29

What if this Christmas season
You help your neighbour in need,
Without looking for an excuse or a reason,
Just to share joy, to plant a good seed.
> Sunday 28.11.2021

December 30

A new year is a new start, –
Just do your part.
Use wisely the present
And the future will not make you resent.
> Sunday 28.11.2021

December 31

A new year is a new life, a new hope.
Treat it as such asking God to help you cope
And showing gratitude to Him and to all.
Smile, believe, stand tall!

Sunday 28.11.2021

Index (tags)

Reader's notes